Lerner SPORTS

SUPER SPORTS
TEAMS

INSIDE THE
DALLAS
COWBOYS

CHRISTINA HILL

T0015693

Lerner Publications ◆ Minneapolis

SPORTS THRILLS *MEET* RESEARCH SKILLS

Lerner **SPORTS**

Free Database Trial: **lernersports.com**

Lerner Publications Company
An imprint of Lerner Publishing Group, Inc.
241 First Avenue North
Minneapolis, MN 55401 USA

For reading levels and more information, look up this title at www.lernerbooks.com.

Main body text set in Aptifer Slab LT Pro / Typeface provided by Linotype AG

Library of Congress Cataloging-in-Publication Data
Names: Hill, Christina, author.
Title: Inside the Dallas Cowboys / Christina Hill.
Description: Minneapolis, MN : Lerner Publications, [2023] | Series: Super Sports Teams (Lerner Sports) | Includes bibliographical references and index. | Audience: Ages 7–11 years | Audience: Grades 4–6 | Summary: "The Dallas Cowboys are nicknamed America's Team, and they're one of the world's most valuable and popular sports teams. Discover the history of this NFL juggernaut and find out what's next for America's Team"— Provided by publisher.
Identifiers: LCCN 2021053172 (print) | LCCN 2021053173 (ebook) | ISBN 9781728458076 (Library Binding) | ISBN 9781728463407 (Paperback) | ISBN 9781728462356 (eBook)
Subjects: LCSH: Dallas Cowboys (Football team)—History—Juvenile literature. | Football players—Texas— Dallas—History—Juvenile literature. | Football—Texas—Dallas—History—Juvenile literature.
Classification: LCC GV956.D3 H55 2023 (print) | LCC GV956.D3 (ebook) | DDC 796.332/64097642812—dc23/eng/20220110

LC record available at https://lccn.loc.gov/2021053172
LC ebook record available at https://lccn.loc.gov/2021053173

TABLE OF CONTENTS

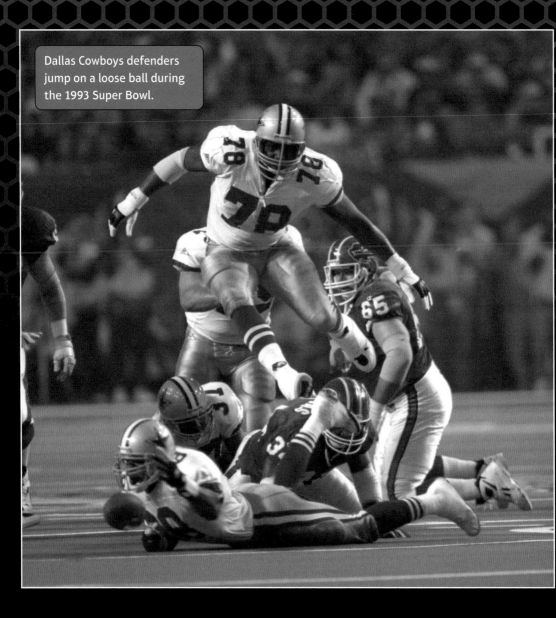

Dallas Cowboys defenders jump on a loose ball during the 1993 Super Bowl.

SUPER BOWL
CHAMPIONS

FACTS AT A GLANCE

- **THE DALLAS COWBOYS** are the most valuable team in the NFL at $6.5 billion.

- The **FEWEST POINTS** ever scored by one team in a Super Bowl game is three. It happened for the first time in 1972, when the Cowboys beat the Miami Dolphins 24–3.

- The Cowboys nickname is **AMERICA'S TEAM** because they are so popular in the US.

- **THE COWBOYS** have played a game on Thanksgiving almost every year since 1966.

In 1993, the Dallas Cowboys beat the Buffalo Bills to win the National Football League (NFL) Super Bowl. But could Dallas repeat their victory and become champions the following year? The two teams faced each other again in the 1994 Super Bowl.

The game began with an exciting kick return of 50 yards by Cowboys player Kevin Williams. Dallas quarterback Troy Aikman continued the strong start with a 20-yard pass to Michael Irvin. But the drive quickly stalled, and the Cowboys had to settle for a 41-yard field goal.

The Bills came back to tie the game in the first quarter with a record-setting 54-yard field goal. In the second quarter, they scored another field goal and a touchdown. The game wasn't looking good for the Cowboys at halftime. They were losing 13–6. The Bills were close to winning their first Super Bowl.

But in the second half, the Cowboys took over. Dallas defender James Washington picked up a fumble. He ran for a touchdown and tied the game. Running back Emmitt Smith carried the ball seven times on an eight-play drive to score. The Cowboys outscored the Bills 24–0 in the second half and won the game 30–13. Smith earned the Most Valuable Player (MVP) award, and the Cowboys won their fourth Super Bowl trophy.

Cowboys defender James Washington carries the ball after an interception in the second half of the 1994 Super Bowl. He also recovered a fumble in the game.

Emmitt Smith ran for 132 yards and scored two touchdowns in the 1994 Super Bowl.

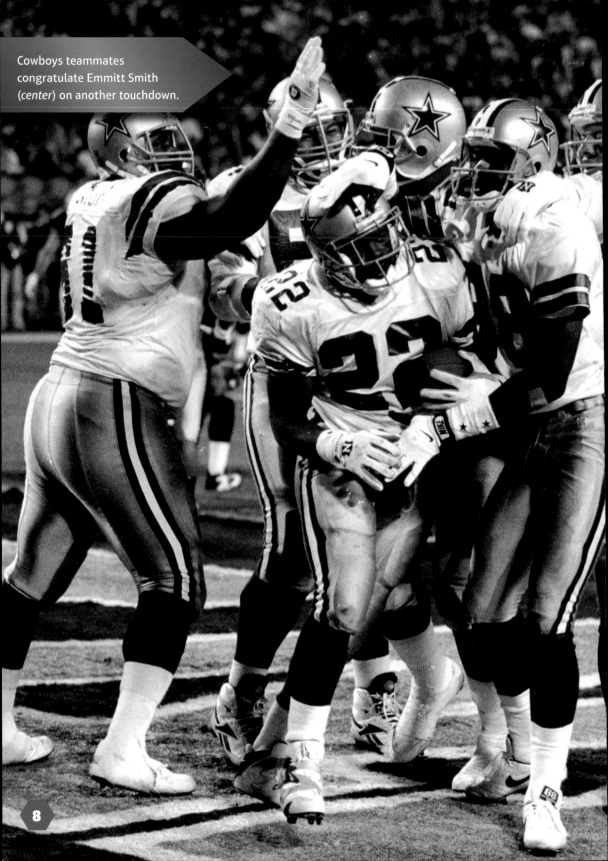

Cowboys teammates congratulate Emmitt Smith (*center*) on another touchdown.

AMERICA'S TEAM

In 1960, the NFL added a new team to the National Football Conference East Division (NFC East). The team was originally called the Dallas Steers. Players weren't too excited to be named after cows, so the team changed its name to the Rangers. Dallas changed again to avoid sharing a name with the Texas Rangers, a professional baseball team. Luckily, the third option stuck. The team officially became the Dallas Cowboys in March of 1960.

Former Cowboys coach Tom Landry (*center*) is one of the NFL's most legendary coaches.

Texas already had two other NFL teams. The Houston Oilers and the Dallas Texans were fan favorites. The Cowboys had to fight to make a name for themselves.

The Cowboys didn't win a single game in their first season. But the team soon proved their talent on the football field. In 1966, the Cowboys began a season winning streak that would last for 20 seasons in a row. Fans all across the US noticed their success and cheered them on. The Cowboys earned the nickname America's Team.

Quarterback Don Meredith played for the Cowboys from 1960 to 1968.

Cowboys owner Jerry Jones is very involved in team decisions.

The Cowboys' first owner was Clint Murchison Jr. He sold the team to Harvey Bright in 1984. Jerry Jones bought the team from Bright in 1989, and he has owned the franchise ever since.

The first Cowboys coach was Tom Landry. Landry remained the team's coach for 29 seasons. After Landry, the team has had eight coaches, including the legendary Jimmy Johnson and current head coach Mike McCarthy.

The Cowboys played at the Cotton Bowl stadium from 1960 to 1970.

The Cowboys started at the Cotton Bowl, a stadium in Dallas. In 1971, they transferred to Texas Stadium in Irving, Texas. In 2009, the team built a new place to play. Jones helped pay for a modern, high-tech home for his team. AT&T Stadium can seat more than 80,000 fans. The stadium's roof can open to let in the sun on good weather days and close to keep out storms.

AT&T Stadium has one of the world's largest video displays to help fans see all the action on the field.

Quarterback Troy Aikman was MVP of the 1993 Super Bowl.

AMAZING MOMENTS

Cowboys history is full of dramatic and entertaining games. They have made it to the Super Bowl eight times. The team became Super Bowl champions in 1972, 1978, 1993, 1994, and 1996.

Not all of their biggest moments ended in victory. Dallas faced the Baltimore Colts in the 1971 Super Bowl. Both teams had a rough game full of penalties and poor plays. The score was tied 13–13 in the fourth quarter. The Colts kicked a 32-yard field goal with only nine seconds remaining to win 16–13.

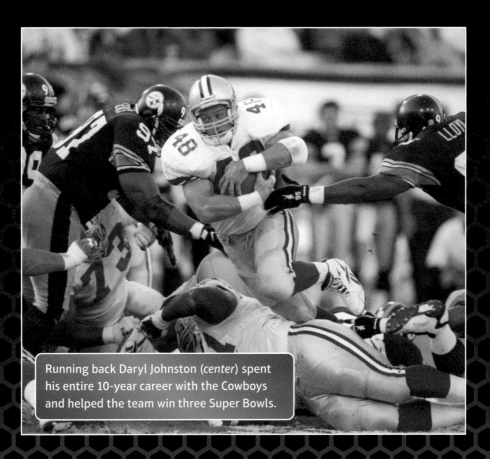

Running back Daryl Johnston (*center*) spent his entire 10-year career with the Cowboys and helped the team win three Super Bowls.

Despite losing, Cowboys linebacker Chuck Howley won the Super Bowl MVP award. He caught two interceptions and recovered a fumble, which set him apart from the other players. Howley is the only person in NFL history to win MVP while being on the losing team.

The Cowboys made it back to the Super Bowl in 1972. They played against the Miami Dolphins in Louisiana. The game was one of the coldest Super Bowls on record. The temperature was only 39°F (4°C).

The Cowboys were determined to overcome the cold and win the Super Bowl. They dominated the game and kept the Dolphins from scoring a single touchdown. With 252 rushing yards and 23 first downs, Dallas put on an amazing show for their fans. The Cowboys won the game 24–3. Dallas was the first Super Bowl team to hold their opponent to just three points. It didn't happen again until the New England Patriots defeated the Los Angeles Rams 13–3 in the 2019 Super Bowl.

After an injury forced him to retire from the NFL after two years with the Chicago Bears, Chuck Howley made a comeback and played another 13 seasons with the Cowboys.

In the 1980s, the San Francisco 49ers dominated the NFL with four Super Bowl wins. Throughout the 1990s, the Cowboys had a rivalry with the 49ers. The rivalry officially began when the two teams faced each other in 1992 for the NFC Championship Game. The 49ers were expected to win. But Dallas fans cheered as Troy Aikman, Michael Irvin, and Emmitt Smith controlled the game for the Cowboys.

Dallas led San Francisco for most of the game and won 30–20. The Cowboys were on their way to the Super Bowl. They crushed the Bills 52–17 for their third Super Bowl victory.

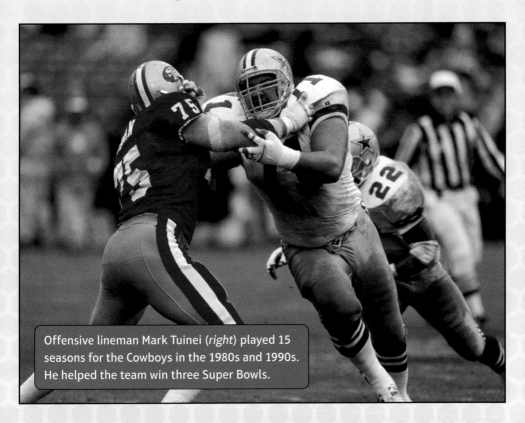

Offensive lineman Mark Tuinei (*right*) played 15 seasons for the Cowboys in the 1980s and 1990s. He helped the team win three Super Bowls.

Michael Irvin is one of the most successful wide receivers in NFL history.

COWBOYS SUPERSTARS

The Cowboys owe their success to superstar players and legendary coaches. Former head coach Tom Landry led the team for 29 seasons. He was creative and invented new ways to play. Landry created the 4–3 defense with four defensive linemen and three linebackers on the field together. The 4–3 defense is still common in the NFL.

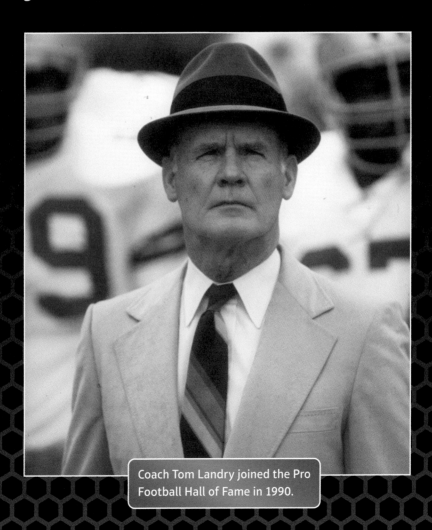

Coach Tom Landry joined the Pro Football Hall of Fame in 1990.

Throughout the team's history, key players have stepped up in the biggest moments. Bob Lilly played tough defense for Dallas from 1961 to 1974. In 1972, he helped the Cowboys win their first Super Bowl. Lilly was also the first Cowboys player to enter the Pro Football Hall of Fame. His superstar moves earned him the nickname Mr. Cowboy.

Roger Staubach was a great Cowboys quarterback who joined the team as a rookie in 1969. He played 11 seasons with the Cowboys and took them to four Super Bowls. Staubach earned the MVP award for the 1972 Super Bowl. Another legendary Cowboy was running back Tony Dorsett. In a 1983 game against the Minnesota Vikings, Dorsett became the first player to run 99 yards to score a touchdown.

Tony Dorsett's 99-yard rushing touchdown against the Minnesota Vikings set an NFL record.

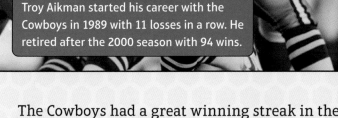

Troy Aikman started his career with the Cowboys in 1989 with 11 losses in a row. He retired after the 2000 season with 94 wins.

The Cowboys had a great winning streak in the 1990s. Quarterback Troy Aikman, wide receiver Michael Irvin, and running back Emmitt Smith led the team on offense. All three players are in the Hall of Fame. Smith was a fan favorite because he excelled at everything on the field. He could run, catch, block, and score. He holds the NFL's all-time career rushing record with 18,355 yards.

In 2003, Tony Romo joined the Cowboys as a backup quarterback. He didn't get a chance to play during his first year. But patience and determination paid off for Romo. In 2006, he threw his first touchdown pass to win a game against the Houston Texans. That moment sparked Romo's successful 13-season career with the Cowboys.

Quarterback Tony Romo holds several Cowboys records, including career passing yards with 34,183.

In 2016, rookie quarterback Dak Prescott joined the Cowboys as a fourth-round draft pick. He expected to be on the bench that season, but Romo and backup Kellen Moore were both injured. Prescott became the starting quarterback. Fans were impressed by the young player's skill. Prescott earned the title of NFL Offensive Rookie of the Year.

Quarterback Dak Prescott is ready to lead the Cowboys back to the Super Bowl.

LET'S GO, COWBOYS!

The Cowboys haven't made it to the Super Bowl since 1996, but that hasn't stopped their millions of fans from filling the stadium or tuning in to their games. In 2020, the Cowboys topped the charts as the most popular NFL team. They are also worth about $6.5 billion, making them the highest valued team in the NFL.

Cowboys fans have plenty of team spirit. Loyal supporters from across the US fill the stands wearing the team colors of navy, silver, and white. They are proud to display the team's famous star logo representing the Texas state nickname, the Lone Star State. The team mascot is a cowboy named Rowdy.

Rowdy has been the official Cowboys mascot since 1996.

The Dallas Cowboys Cheerleaders are one of the most famous cheerleading squads in the NFL. They boost the energy of the fans and cheer on the team. The cheerleaders also focus on helping people. They often visit US military groups around the world. The Cowboys Cheerleaders partnered with the Salvation Army in 1997. Since then, the cheerleaders have helped raise millions of dollars. The Salvation Army uses the money to provide meals to people in need.

The Cowboys are known for playing a game every year on Thanksgiving Day. Family, feasts, and football are American traditions that fans look forward to each year on the fourth Thursday in November. This could be a big reason why the Cowboys remain America's Team.

The Cowboys are working hard to return to the Super Bowl. Their future looks bright. The team hired its ninth head coach in 2020, former Super Bowl-winning coach Mike McCarthy. Dak Prescott signed a contract in 2021 to stay with the team for four more years. Fans hope that their beloved team will secure a sixth Super Bowl victory in the near future.

Ezekiel Elliott (*center*) has finished five seasons ranked in the NFL's top 10 for rushing yards since his career began in 2016.

Mike McCarthy spent 13 seasons as head coach of the Green Bay Packers before taking over for the Cowboys.

Jason Witten's 18 catches in the October 28, 2012, game against the New York Giants is a Cowboys record.

COWBOYS
SEASON RECORD HOLDERS

RUSHING TOUCHDOWNS

1. Emmitt Smith, 25 (1995)
2. Emmitt Smith, 21 (1994)
3. Emmitt Smith, 18 (1992)
4. Ezekiel Elliott, 15 (2016)
5. Marion Barber, 14 (2006)

RECEIVING TOUCHDOWNS

1. Dez Bryant, 16 (2014)
2. Terrell Owens, 15 (2007)
3. Frank Clarke, 14 (1962)
4. Dez Bryant, 13 (2013)
5. Bob Hayes, 13 (1966)

PASSING YARDS

1. Tony Romo, 4,903 (2012)
2. Dak Prescott, 4,902 (2019)
3. Tony Romo, 4,483 (2009)
4. Tony Romo, 4,211 (2007)
5. Tony Romo, 4,184 (2011)

RUSHING YARDS

1. DeMarco Murray, 1,845 (2014)
2. Emmitt Smith, 1,773 (1995)
3. Emmitt Smith, 1,713 (1992)
4. Tony Dorsett, 1,646 (1981)
5. Ezekiel Elliott, 1,631 (2016)

PASS CATCHES

1. Michael Irvin, 111 (1995)
2. Jason Witten, 110 (2012)
3. Jason Witten, 96 (2007)
4. Jason Witten, 94 (2009)
5. Jason Witten, 94 (2010)

SACKS

1. DeMarcus Ware, 20 (2008)
2. DeMarcus Ware, 19.5 (2011)
3. DeMarcus Ware, 15.5 (2010)
4. DeMarcus Lawrence, 14.5 (2017)
5. Jim Jeffcoat, 14 (1986)

GLOSSARY

defensive lineman: a defender who usually plays at the front of the defense near the line of scrimmage

draft: when teams take turns choosing new players

drive: a series of plays

field goal: a score of three points made by kicking the football between the goalposts

franchise: a team that is a member of a professional sports league

fumble: when a football player loses hold of the ball while handling or running with it

interception: a pass caught by the defending team that results in a change of possession

linebacker: a defender who usually plays in the middle of the defense

rivalry: when a player or team tries to defeat or be more successful than another

rookie: a first-year player

wide receiver: a player whose main job is to catch passes

LEARN MORE

Coleman, Ted. *Dallas Cowboys*. Mendota Heights, MN: Press Room Editions, 2021.

Dallas Cowboys
https://www.dallascowboys.com

Dallas Cowboys Hall of Famers
https://www.profootballhof.com/teams/dallas-cowboys/

Fishman, Jon M. *Dak Prescott*. Minneapolis: Lerner Publications, 2019.

Fishman, Jon M. *Ezekiel Elliott*. Minneapolis: Lerner Publications, 2018.

Sports Illustrated Kids—Football
https://www.sikids.com/football

INDEX

PHOTO ACKNOWLEDGMENTS

Image credits: Rick Stewart/Stringer/Getty Images, p.4; George Rose/Stringer/Getty Images, p.6; Rick Stewart/Stringer/Getty Images, p.7; John Green/UPI Photo Service/Newscom, p.8; Otto Greule Jr/Stringer/Getty Images, p.9; Michael Ochs Archives/Handout/Getty Images, p.10; Thearon W. Henderson/Stringer/Getty Images, p.11; jmanaugh3/Shutterstock, p.12; Tim Warner/Stringer/Getty Images, p.13; Stephen Dunn/Staff/Getty Images, p.14; Rick Stewart/Stringer/Getty Images, p.15; Fma12/Wikimedia, p.16; George Rose/Stringer/Getty Images, p.17; Al Golub/ZUMA Press/Newscom, p.18; Stephen Dunn/Staff/Getty Images, p.19; Rick Stewart/Stringer/Getty Images, p.20; Rick Stewart/Stringer/Getty Images, p.21; Tom Pennington/Staff/Getty Images, p.22; Ronald Martinez/Staff/Getty Images, p.23; Richard Rodriguez/Stringer/Getty Images, p.24; Ronald Martinez/Staff/Getty Images, p.25; Wesley Hitt/Stringer/Getty Images, p.26; Christian Petersen/Staff/Getty Images, p.27; Ronald Martinez/Staff/Getty Images, p.28;

Design element: Master3D/Shutterstock.com.

Cover image: Ronald Martinez/Staff/Getty Images